142 Evangelism Ideas for Your Church

142 Evangelism Ideas for Your Church

Larry Moyer
and
Cameron D. Abell
–Editors–

Foreword by Haddon W. Robinson

BAKER BOOK HOUSE
Grand Rapids, Michigan 49516

CONTENTS

Foreword

Several years ago, an advertiser faced the truth about his merchandise. "We couldn't improve the product, so we improved the box." That strategy also applies to the gospel of Jesus Christ.

In other words, don't tamper with the message, but take a look at the package in which you offer it. Bringing women and men to the Savior demands that we present the basic content in different ways to meet different needs in different situations.

Larry Moyer and Cam Abell offer a variety of ideas—some old, some new, but all tested—to attract people in our society to hear the great news about Jesus. All of these suggestions are usable. If some seem like keen insight into the obvious, don't dismiss them out of hand. It's astonishing how well ordinary ideas work for those who decide to work them!

If church leaders discover only ten ideas in this book that they can use and then practice them, their congregations will experience the invigoration of evangelism—that's a bargain at any price.

Haddon W. Robinson
President, Denver Seminary

A Word of Thanks

To the many pastors and other church leaders who took the time and interest to respond to us and share the ideas they've found effective.

To Cam Abell, staff evangelist with EvanTell, who spent hours cataloging and refining the ideas to list them in such a way that both the principle behind the idea and the "how to" could be easily grasped by the reader.

We appreciate what you've done so that multitudes of lost people might be reached for the Savior.

A Word of Explanation

For those of you not familiar with EvanTell, this association is committed to expository evangelism characterized by a clear presentation of the gospel of grace and a clear explanation of the biblical text. Staff members conduct evangelistic crusades, disciple ministerial students interested in evangelism, and prepare materials to assist in evangelistic efforts.

Introduction

When asked, "What is the best way to reach the masses?" D. L. Moody answered, "Go for them!"

Consistently evangelistic churches are those who "go for them." Their leaders and their lay people recognize that there is one message (Christ died for our sins and arose), but a variety of methods whereby that message may be communicated to a lost person. As Arthur P. Johnston expressed in *The Battle for World Evangelism*, "Methods of evangelism are as diverse as those who are to be reached, and as those that reach them" (p. 207).

Recognizing the many ways by which the unsaved can be approached with the gospel, EvanTell wrote to over two thousand church leaders and asked them to share any idea they had found effective in evangelism. The response was encouraging. Within several weeks a couple of hundred ideas were received.

We share these with you with two goals in mind. First, that you might know what other brothers and sisters in Christ have found effective. Not all of the ideas will work in your community, but many of them will.

Second, our hope is that these ideas will be a springboard to cause you to think of ways you may have overlooked to reach the lost. They are not meant to be an end in themselves but to stimulate you to do your own brainstorming. We believe these ideas will encourage you to buy up every opportunity to influence the unsaved for Christ as Paul admonished the Colossians (Col. 4:5). You will notice that not every idea gives you an immediate opportunity to present the gospel. Some simply establish the basis from which you can come back and present the gospel later.

In keeping with the purpose of this book, we have limited the ideas to those which the church as a corporate body of believers can use in reaching the lost. However, a church follows its pastor. In order for a church to be evangelistic, the pastor must be an example—not merely an exhorter in evangelism. Therefore, at the end of the book, we have included ten ideas a pastor can use to be an example to his people in reaching those without Christ.

May God use the ideas presented here to cause

every church exposed to them to pledge before God that they will use every means possible to reach the lost in their community for Christ.

Larry Moyer, Executive Director
EvanTell, Inc.

Part 1

*Activities Directly
Associated with
the Church*

1

Using Classes During the Sunday School Hour

To homes in your area send a book (*Strike the Original Match* by Charles R. Swindoll [Portland, Ore.: Multnomah Press, 1980], *Dare to Discipline* by James Dobson [Wheaton, Tyndale, 1973]) that hits a need unsaved people have. Invite them to attend a class on the topic using the book.

Teach a class called "Foundations of Christianity," part of which obviously includes the gospel message. Urge members to invite their non-Christian friends.

Hold an inquirer's class for interested people. Use it to address questions unsaved people have.

Example: "How do we know there is a God?" "How can a loving God send people to hell?" "Why is there so much suffering in the world?" "Can you know for sure you are going to heaven?"

Have a Sunday school class just for newcomers who bring their children to church but do not ordinarily stay. They feel less threatened being together than by being in a class with others who "know a lot about the Bible."

2

Using the Church Service

Have church members give testimonies at services to reach the unsaved. Select those who make the gospel clear and relate well to their friends and associates. For their benefit and yours, have them write out their testimony and share it with you before giving it. Give them feedback that will help them enhance the communication of their testimony when they give it in public.

Have special, evangelistic services at times such as Christmas Eve, Easter, Mother's Day, Father's Day, graduation, and so forth. Use high-quality special music and sing familiar songs. Have no offering. Serve refreshments after the sevice.

Conduct a week-long evangelistic crusade. Using an evangelist who is clear on the gospel, address the unsaved at each service. Start your preparation a year in advance, especially instructing the people on how to build relationships with their lost friends. As with other outreaches, the leaders' excitement and example in bringing the unsaved is a key to the success of the week.

Have a "Friend Day" in the church. For three months ahead of this, encourage the people to build relationships and invite their friends to this service. Present Christ as the one whose reputation was that of "a friend of sinners." Visit those who attended the service the weeks following.

Once a quarter have a special Sunday service that would appeal to the unsaved. Everything from the music to the message should be directed to the unsaved. Prepare your messages with the unsaved in mind, using clear terminology and helpful illustrations. Provide an attractive flyer for guests to introduce a special or new preaching series. Consider topics such as "Do you have to be good to get to heaven?" or "How do you know Jesus Christ was who he said he was?" or messages that address current issues such as abortion, AIDS, pornography, stress, and family relationships. Explain passages that speak to these areas and show how these are symptoms of a deeper need met through the gospel. Consider canceling Sunday school that morning to make it easier for believers to bring their friends with them to the service. Encourage them to invite the unsaved to dinner afterward.

Have a special service recognizing children in a particular ministry of the church and invite their parents. For example, have a youth Sunday. Invite parents to the service with a potluck to follow. Use the opportunity to explain Christ's concern for both children and parents.

In camping or resort areas, hold an outdoor service on the front lawn of the church inviting vacationers to join you. Use a microphone to allow easier hearing. Provide for fellowship afterward.

3

Using Other
Church Ministries

Conduct Vacation Bible School (VBS) at night and provide an outreach for the parents as well as the children. Consider having women call the parents during VBS and thank them for sending their children. Invite them to attend a closing program and to help by bringing a small dessert. Include a gospel message and end with a social to meet the visitors.

Send a letter to the parents of children who attended VBS. Give each an evangelistic booklet that is attractive and intriguing. EvanTell has three available: "How Do You Know When You're Good Enough to Get to Heaven?" "Can You Be Sure You

Are Going to Heaven?" and "What Do You Have to Do to Get to Heaven?" The letter should thank them for allowing their children to attend your VBS and call attention to the booklet you're sending as a gift.

Have a yearly film series in place of evening services and invite the unsaved to attend. Give out tickets to neighbors and friends and train counselors to respond to those in need. You may even want to rent a theater and invite all church members to attend with their friends. Use films such as *Caught, Twice Pardoned, Cry Upon the Mountain,* and *Turn Your Heart Toward Home.*

Use children's ministries as a bridge to reach the parents. Visit in the homes and invite the parents to special services.

4

Special Activities

Run a summer day camp at the church with the kids preparing an evangelistic play or musical to be given at the end of the week. Have a barbecue for the family prior to the program.

Hold a September fair on the church grounds or in a nearby park. Have crafts, booths, hot-air balloon rides, children's festival, and so forth. It is a festive event and may or may not include a gospel message. Use the opportunity to develop contacts with those you can visit and perhaps evangelize later.

Sponsor a lock in/lock out for youth in the congregation and have them invite their unsaved friends. Parents can socialize during this time in one location, while the youth stay overnight at the church and have activities. Have a dynamic youth speaker to interact with the young people and answer questions. Use the opportunity to present the gospel.

Have a special emphasis such as a game night, oriental potluck, or Mexican fiesta. Invite interested people in the community and follow up on visitors afterwards.

Invite a professional theater company to present at the church a series of dramas designed to reach the lost. Publicize it thoroughly.

Have a regular sixty-second spot on a local radio station designed to give a relevant and thought-provoking idea from Scripture. Make it positive, warm, and inviting. It need not necessarily invite the public to the services. The regular exposure of the pastor's name, the name of the church, and the phone number will be sufficient. Do offer to be of assistance at any time. Attempt to secure a time when most people will be tuned in to their radios. Even if substantial expense is involved, it will be worth at least a trial period.

Part 2

Activities Related to Door-to-Door Evangelism

5

Establishing Sources for Contacts

In the services use response slips for people to express interest in having a visit from someone in the church.

Have immediate and low-key follow-up of church visitors by Operation Heartbeat. Call visitors on Sunday afternoon or evening and set a time to visit. Or, have church leaders designated to drop by the homes of visitors on the way home after the service for a brief *at-the-door* visit and to leave literature expressing your gratefulness for having them with you. A follow-up visit could be made later.

Express a thank-you to visitors with a gift item such as a book, baked goods, directory of services in the community, and so forth. Use the opportunity to determine interest in a future visit where the gospel may be discussed.

After an Easter or Christmas cantata or drama visit guests who have attended.

Conduct a telemarketing survey and invite people to special services such as Easter or services addressing special needs, issues, or concerns.

Visit newcomers in your area by obtaining lists from the Water Department or Chamber of Commerce. Extend a welcome to the community and an invitation to the church, leaving a brochure giving the times of services. If practical, include a gift item as a token of friendship.

Send thank-you letters to anyone visiting or to parents sending children to the church and follow the letters with a visit.

Visit homes of children who attended a ministry of the church. Assign names to church members in their area.

Using the newspaper, record families who have had a baby and send them a card at the time of birth. Follow with a phone call or visit to invite them to a special family-oriented activity such as a Dobson video. You may want to send a gift book on child-rearing from a Christian perspective to each home within a particular radius of the church. Accompany the book with a letter from the pastor, expressing the church's interest in the family and offer to be of assistance whenever needed. You might call a month or two later and ask if it would be possible to come by and meet them.

Include information about your church in the Welcome Wagon packet and follow up with a visit to welcome new neighbors and assist them in any way possible.

Visit every home in the community. Place hangers on the door with a survey, church brochure, and attractive evangelistic booklet. Ask each resident to place the survey back on the door to be picked up at a designated time. Use the survey to discern their interest in spiritual matters.

Place attractive evangelistic booklets near the door of the church for visitors to take and church members to distribute. Call attention to them and give the church members ideas on how and when to use them. Be sure the material gives a clear presentation of the gospel.

Use the phone directory to send about one hundred letters a week (or whatever number is practical) to people in the community with the thrust, WE ARE YOUR NEIGHBOR. Have a team follow up on these letters with a phone call and visit those interested.

Develop and conduct a community survey to discern people's interest in spiritual matters. Offer to respond to each participant with the results of the survey. Be alert to those willing and interested in talking in depth about their personal need of Christ.

Send tapes (on marriage or a children's tape with songs and stories) to individuals in the community you have reason to feel would be interested. Enclose a description of church activities.

Have a citywide telephone campaign, keeping a list of receptive people and encouraging someone to visit them.

Set aside one Sunday evening to do formal visitation in the community using church brochures. Invite those contacted to attend if they don't have a church home.

Send a monthly letter or newspaper to residents in the area. Have short, interesting articles, focusing on biblical solutions to pertinent problems. Use it as a preevangelism tool to establish relationships and develop rapport with the lost. Articles should include a mixture of living the Christian life as well as those with an evangelistic approach. The newspaper can also include coupons which people return to obtain books or home Bible studies.

Offer to the public high-quality videos dealing with marriage, finances, or relationships to build bridges. Offers can be made through the radio or newspaper.

Develop an information packet that provides helpful information for newcomers who have moved to your community. The last page or section contains information about your church. Distribute this door-to-door and use a follow-up questionnaire to tactfully turn the conversation to spiritual matters and present the gospel.

Part 3

*Activities Related
to Outreach Studies*

6

Types of Groups

Have neighborhood Bible studies and invite friends and neighbors to attend. These may be topic oriented ("Who is Christ?" "Can I trust the Bible?"), book oriented (a study through John), or need oriented (happiness, loneliness, boredom, and so forth).

Conduct Bible studies for senior citizens twice a month. Have lunch from 12:00-1:00 and a study from 1:00-2:00 in John's Gospel. It would probably be best not to use study guides, but it should be a guided discussion.

Have a Bible study for international students and share the gospel as time and study permits.

7

Topic Oriented Activities

Plan regular discussion groups to which unsaved people can come and ask any questions they want about the Bible. A capable leader answers the questions with a fellowship time afterward.

Have a series on commonly asked questions by non-Christians to which they are invited to discuss thoughts, concerns, or objections regarding life and the Bible.

Hold evangelistic Bible studies with one or two couples providing the nucleus, and inviting their friends through a written invitation and a phone call to a four- to six-week study on prophecy, John 1-3, "Who is God?" "What is man's problem?" "What is God's solution?" or answers to questions they may have.

Provide Bible studies at the church dealing with parenting, temperaments, or emotions. Cover topics such as how to manage money, how to handle marital conflicts, or how to have a happy family. Don't necessarily hide the fact that it is a church-sponsored study. That could be helpful in giving it credibility.

Invite people to attend a Bible study on some current issue such as abortion, euthanasia, capital punishment, and so forth.

Begin a four-to six-week Bible study after a New Year's gathering, centering around the scriptural plan for families.

Offer a ten-week Bible walk-through study taught by church people.

Part 4

*Activities to Reach
Specific Groups of People*

8

Children

Organize a T-ball league for kindergarten children. Use the practice sessions to build relationships with non-Christian parents with whom believers can share the gospel.

Have a mission on wheels using a van or mobile unit where workers go to a section of town, inviting children door-to-door to attend a program with puppets, flannelgraph, music, singing, and storytelling.

Have a puppet show designed to introduce children to the gospel. Consider using a park and having the show taped for a local TV station.

Host Five-Day Clubs to reach children in the community.

As part of a bus ministry, invite the children and their parents to a dinner with a light program to acquaint parents with the church.

Have an after-school program for elementary school children, providing extended day-care.

9

Youth

Sponsor a youth camp with expenses paid for those who cannot afford it. It may be targeted to reach those in the inner-city area.

Have an after-church singspiration for young people and incorporate testimonies and a devotional. Develop the format of the evening with unsaved youth specifically in mind.

Have a youth all-nighter from 5:00 P.M. to 7:00 A.M. with a progressive dinner, bowling, VCR movies, breakfast, and devotional.

The youth pastor can meet individually with every young person in the church yearly to discuss the gospel, assurance, and their Christian walk.

Provide a weekend retreat for young people where they can have fun and hear an informal presentation of the gospel.

Consider previewing a football action film like *More Than Winning* with the coach in town and get his reaction. It may be possible to invite a team over to see the film. Use the opportunity to express appreciation to the coach and team for what they mean to the community.

Have a night dealing with a topic of special interest to youth. For example, use Josh McDowell's material from *Why Wait* (San Bernardino, Calif.: Here's Life, 1989) as a means of ministering to them and then present the gospel.

Have regular "fireside chats" in your home and encourage the church youth to invite their unsaved friends. As you discuss subjects of interest to them, be open to opportunities to present the gospel.

During football season have a fifth quarter for young people and adults after the game. Use separate locations for the two groups. It is best to have it in a home and provide refreshments. If a Christian athlete is available to give a testimony, have him or her do so. If not, just some time for interaction and games will offer meaningful contact with the unsaved.

For high school graduation provide a Sunday morning free breakfast for graduates and their parents and have Christian coaches or players give their testimonies. Afterward, a special class could be offered for the seniors and another for parents. Recognize all of the guests in the service.

10

Men

Have retreats where unsaved are invited. Plan time for leisure, seminars, and fellowship. Use the time to build relationships with the unsaved in a nonthreatening atmosphere.

In the spring and fall, sponsor a men's golf tournament to which each man brings an unsaved friend. Give away trophies and humorous prizes. Follow with a meal and message.

Once a month have a Friday-night-men's dinner at the church, cooked by men, for men, to reach men. Have a believer with a clear testimony whose name or work is prominent in the community share details of his work and how he came to know the

Savior. (A church that did this regularly had its highest attendance when a Christian FBI agent was invited to speak.)

Build relationships with unsaved men by encouraging them to become part of the church softball or basketball team. A couples' volleyball team may also work well in your community.

Schedule a men's breakfast four times a year and bring in an athlete, doctor, lawyer, ex-convict, scientist, and so forth to give his testimony.

Cooperate with other churches for a men's breakfast that involves testimonies and a good speaker.

Have a men's luncheon. Address topics of interest such as something related to financial planning, the efficient use of time, stress management, or developing parenting skills. Invite an individual respected in the community to give testimony. Make sure the event is well organized.

Have a yearly father and son canoe trip, inviting unsaved friends to attend. During the camp-out, include a devotional focused on the gospel.

In January host a wild-game feed for the men, potluck style, with men preparing the meal. The dishes should be identified with the cook's name and the type of meat. Have entertainment and an interesting speaker who will give the gospel message.

Play pick-up basketball in a local gym and have the men invite the unsaved to come. Schedule it at 9:00 P.M. so you will not pull fathers away from young children.

Sponsor a pizza night at a pizza parlor. Rent a room or the entire restaurant and show a video like *Football Fever* or *NFL Follies* to men and their sons. Have a football player give his testimony and a gospel message.

Hold a weekly men's luncheon with a low-priced but good meal from 11:45-12:45. Use the first half for eating and the last half for Bible study. Mail out letters but stress personal invitations.

Hold a burger banquet with a speaker that would appeal to the group and/or a video on "How to bring in the big ones." Follow this with a bass tournament using outside judging.

Have a father-and-son-day event such as hiking or fishing and have several of the Christian men share their testimony.

Have a men's sports night at a local gym with an intermission for them to hear testimonies and perhaps an informal presentation of the gospel.

Have a salmon bake after a fishing derby at the close of the season. Provide full dinners for anyone who wishes to attend. Follow through on those visiting.

11

Women

Sponsor a yearly "Strawberry Tea" for women, complete with china, silver, and semi-formal dress. The women of the church can provide strawberry desserts, and the program may include a fashion show, crafts, music, door prize, and so forth. Include a tactful presentation of the gospel.

Use friendship Bible coffees to reach unsaved women interested in studying the Scriptures.

Have a "Mother's Day Out" program where free child-care is provided from 9:00 A.M. to 2:00 P.M. for mothers of preschool children. The frequency will depend upon available workers. Use the opportunity to build relationships with unsaved women.

Have a women's luncheon or banquet at a nice restaurant. Invite unsaved friends. Address a concern of common interest to women (cooking, time-management, fashion design, childrearing, and so forth). Invite an individual respected in the community to give testimony. Make sure the event is well organized.

Have a M.O.P.S. (Mothers Of Pre-Schoolers) ministry where those in the church are invited and encouraged to invite unsaved friends. A program (crafts, music, and Bible lesson) is provided for the children while the mothers have a meeting.

For those about to have children: Invite those in a prenatal class to a discussion of the moral and spiritual development of a child or Ross Campbell's book *How to Really Love Your Child* (N.Y.: New American Library, 1982). Once relationships are established, you can springboard from this to a Bible study.

Have women's retreats where the unsaved are invited. Plan time for leisure, seminars, and fellowship. Use the time to build relationships with the unsaved in an enjoyable and nonthreatening atmosphere.

Have an annual mother-daughter banquet and use it to introduce women to spiritual matters.

12

Singles and Career

Sponsor a camp each year for college-age and career people with a program that appeals to their needs.

Sponsor group meetings geared toward singles called F.E.D. (Friday Evening Discussions), centered around topics such as stress management, finances, or dating. Select speakers respected in their area who will give an effective testimony and make the gospel clear.

13

Families

Sponsor a church friendship dinner at a nice restaurant—the more formal the better. Each person who attends must bring an unsaved person or couple with them and pay their way. Have a light time of singing and entertainment (ventriloquist, music, and so forth) and an evangelistic speaker to give a message.

Have Sunday-night-caring groups hold block parties with games and refreshments, inviting the unsaved to attend.

Organize a six-week-volleyball league, having church couples invite unsaved visitors. Use it as an informal way to meet couples and single parents. Hold a potluck banquet at the end and follow-up on those who appear interested in talking about spiritual things.

Sponsor a musical concert at a neutral location. Have local Christian businesses underwrite the event and have extensive advertising. Allow musicians to give testimonies at intermission; evangelistic literature may be given out afterward at an autograph table.

Provide a skating night at a roller rink. If appropriate, include an evangelistic message during the lunch following the skating.

Sponsor a volleyball game. Encourage each person to bring a non-Christian. Don't put undue pressure upon yourself to have an evangelistic message at the game. The contact with believers and a wholesome time may make the unsaved very receptive to an invitation to attend a church service or welcome a visit to their home. Recognize that best results may be seen after doing this several times.

Rent a booth at the local or regional fair and provide evangelistic tracts for those interested. Set up a booth providing ice water for the people. When they come by, give them literature on issues of special interest (parenting, time management, finances, and so forth) as well as the Gospel of John. Consider using surveys to move into the gospel. Invite them to a special service at church.

Have a yearly barbecue and invite the community to attend so they can relate to your people informally.

Invite someone from the Sheriff's Department to join you for a Home Safety potluck. Other possiblities include fire prevention, child safety, and drug prevention. Invite outsiders, especially single parents, with whom you can build relationships.

Challenge your local fire department to a softball game, followed by a cookout to express appreciation to firemen. The same could be done for the police force, city council, and so forth. Schedule it prior to a special evangelistic event the public will be invited to attend.

Sponsor an after-school day-care center for elementary school children whose parents work. Follow up by inviting parents to special programs and church-sponsored dinners.

Have a key Christian speaker hold a sports clinic (golf, tennis, jogging, and so forth) with instruction and a testimony. Follow up on interested people.

Rent a big screen TV and show the Super Bowl at the church. Send out printed invitations and have a key athlete speak at halftime, giving his testimony.

Hold a community activity such as a film or puppet show in a neutral location and invite the unsaved. After the gospel is presented, the believers can interact with their friends and solicit their thoughts.

Set up a booth in a shopping mall once a week where people can come—unsolicited—to interact about spiritual matters and ask questions. Use laypersons to staff the booth.

Hold a yearly family conference with an evangelistic focus. Promote this through leaflets, mailing, and personal contact.

If possible, during a missions conference obtain permission for the missionaries to show slides and artifacts in local schools to enrich pupils' knowledge of the country. No mention of the Christian character of the work will be allowed. However, students may be told of after-school meetings at the church involving songs, games, and a gospel message.

Cooperate with other evangelical churches for an outdoor worship service in a park with an outside speaker.

Have a regular "Friendship Dinner" with a good meal and program to which church people invite their unsaved friends. If possible, reserve a room in a restaurant a minimum of thirty miles from the homes to allow time for interaction on the way home. Christians should pick up their guests and pay for their meals.

Have a special seminar dealing with critical family topics such as parenting, finances, or estate planning. (Example: "Making My Will" seminar with the speaker a qualified attorney from the church.) Use the opportunity to explain how the Scriptures relate to these areas.

Sponsor an evangelistic picnic asking each family to invite another family to join them. Have time for the families to be together and have a few organized group activities, particularly for the children.

14

People with Special Needs

Visit homes of those requesting financial assistance, using the opportunity to show genuine concern and share the gospel.

Obtain names of needy families from social services and take them food and clothing. (Some stores will donate clothes for you to give to the needy.) Build on the relationship and share the gospel with them.

Provide a free spring brunch to senior citizens with special music, an entertaining program, and a short gospel message.

Begin a bereavement support group for families who have recently lost someone in death, such as a Widowed Fellowship.

Provide a support group with a counselor for unwed and/or single mothers.

Put together project teams of youth and adults that will do construction, repair, painting, cleaning, gardening, or cooking for the needy. Use the relationships established to evangelize.

Form a Divorce Recovery Group for those who have been divorced.

Establish a deaf ministry in the church with signing at worship services and Sunday school classes. Have visitation for the deaf.

Begin an "Adopt a Grandparent" ministry which helps the church to care for elderly people. Provide for them at special times of the year and seek to share the gospel with them.

Provide encouragement through testimonies from believers. As time progresses, provide biblical input to minister to their spiritual needs.

Begin a support and counseling group for the visually impaired called VISA (Visually Impaired Support Association).

Start an International Student Fellowship on a local campus for foreign students living in your area. Establish host families to help meet their needs.

Tutor needy children and youth at a local Christian center and use the contacts for evangelism.

Have youth visit a retirement center to sing, play board games, and build bridges that will allow them to present the gospel.

Start an English-as-a-Second-Language program for foreigners and use it as an opportunity to share the gospel.

Part 5

*Activities
for Holidays and
Special Occasions*

15

Christmas

Encourage your families to have Christmas coffees in their homes and invite neighbors to bring a favorite cookie recipe. Discuss Christmas traditions and close by reading the Christmas story and giving a personal testimony of what Christmas means to you. Give each family a New Testament as they leave.

At Christmastime women invite friends to a tea or coffee in their homes. Have one person give an effective testimony and another a clear gospel message at each "tea."

The first Saturday in December host a women's Christmas tea at the church. The ladies invite unsaved guests to attend and an evangelistic message is given.

Re-enact the Christmas scene on the church grounds, inviting the unsaved to attend.

Host a dinner theater during Christmas and Easter seasons and invite the community. Try to keep the cost minimal, having Christians pay for their unsaved guests.

16

Easter

Show a special, quality-produced film dealing with the death and resurrection of Christ annually on Good Friday. After the film offer an attractive booklet that clearly explains the gospel and includes a response card to determine those with further interest. Visit those who respond. (By making this an annual event, some churches have attracted many from their community.)

Run a day-camp in the mornings during Easter week to draw children in for games, songs, and a message. Have young people help with a program supervised by adults.

Have an artist in the church present the life of Christ in life-size art during Easter week and publicize it to draw people to the church to be exposed to the gospel.

17

Thanksgiving

Hold a Thanksgiving supper for the community, asking each person to bring some type of food (which makes them more likely to come). You may want to hold it in a neutral location and have a program afterward.

18

Mother's Day

Offer to take family pictures at the church and encourage people to invite unsaved friends.

19

Valentine's Day

Have a sweetheart banquet with the unsaved invited. Have a meal, skit, music, and speaker.

Hold an annual valentine banquet at a hotel. Bring in a well- known speaker and include a musical or dramatic program that will appeal to non-Christians.

20

Halloween

Distribute door-to-door or mail a small paper sack to homes in the neighborhoods with the time, location, and date of a Halloween activity printed on it. Have games and get addresses of all attending. Use a questionnaire to determine spiritual interests.

Part 6

Personal Evangelism Suggestions for Pastors

Invite several unsaved acquaintances to study a book of the Bible, reviewing a chapter a week. After a few weeks the gospel is shared with each one.

Visit several homes each week introducing yourself and giving information about the church and an evangelistic booklet. Follow up positive visits with a personal letter.

Systematically visit members of your congregation to find out where they are spiritually and share the gospel with other family members who do not know Christ.

Use counseling sessions as a way of reaching couples with the gospel.

Have meals in the homes of your people and encourage them to invite an unsaved couple(s) to attend.

Invite all potential new members and new contacts to your home for a sit-down dinner to get to know them better.

Invite an unsaved man to be your guest for lunch. Consider a non-Christian printer, building contractor, or Sunday-morning visitor. Men often open up about spiritual concerns across a table away from their wives and families.

Join the local YMCA or a local civic group as a means of getting to know unsaved people whom you can evangelize.

Invite unsaved men to participate with you in golf, tennis, fishing, or jogging as a means of building rapport and introducing them to Christ.

Ask a businessman to have a Bible study in his complex, using you as the teacher. Have him invite his unsaved associates to attend.